Daniel Boone

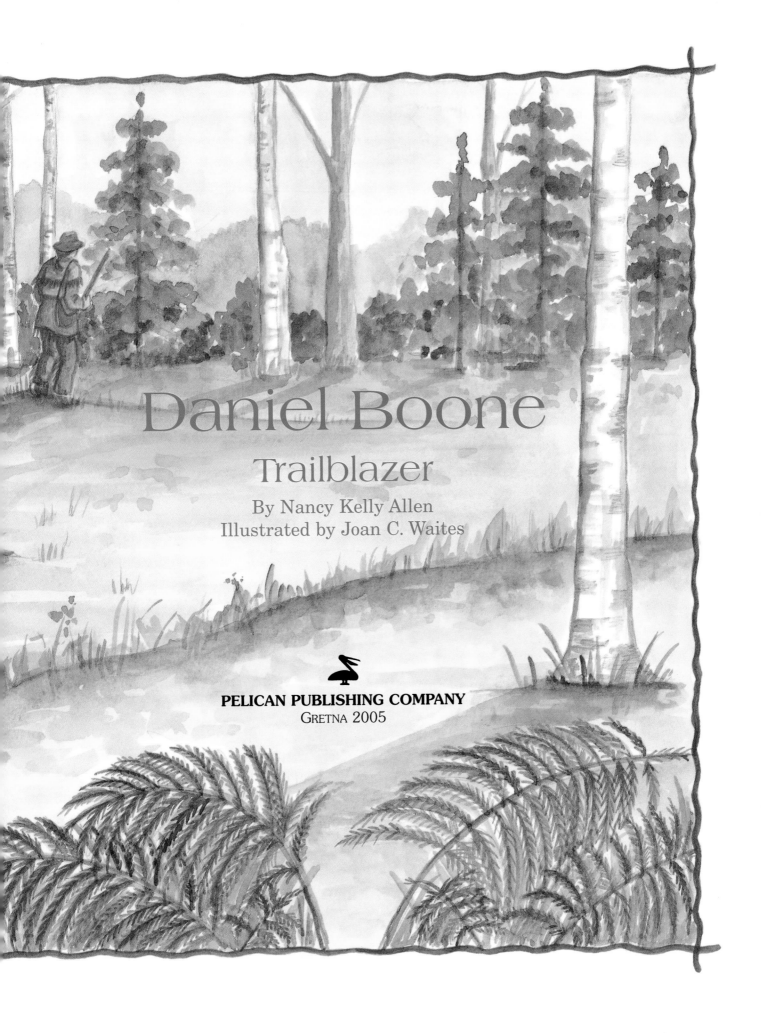

Daniel Boone

Trailblazer

By Nancy Kelly Allen
Illustrated by Joan C. Waites

PELICAN PUBLISHING COMPANY

GRETNA 2005

For Ronald and Velma

*The word "Pelican" and the depiction of a pelican are trademarks
of Pelican Publishing Company, Inc., and are registered in the
U.S. Patent and Trademark Office.*

Library of Congress Cataloging-in-Publication Data

Allen, Nancy Kelly, 1949-
    Daniel Boone : trailblazer / by Nancy Kelly Allen ; illustrated by Joan C. Waites.
        p. cm.
    ISBN-13: 978-1-58980-212-4 (alk. paper)
    1. Boone, Daniel, 1734-1820—Juvenile literature. 2. Pioneers—Kentucky—Biography—Juvenile literature. 3. Explorers—Kentucky—Biography—Juvenile literature. 4. Frontier and pioneer life—Kentucky—Juvenile literature. 5. Kentucky—Biography—Juvenile literature. 6. Kentucky—Discovery and exploration—Juvenile literature. I. Waites, Joan C., ill. II. Title.

    F454.B66A44 2005
    976.9'02'092—dc22

                                                            2004031086

Printed in Singapore

Published by Pelican Publishing Company, Inc.
1000 Burmaster Street, Gretna, Louisiana 70053

DANIEL BOONE: TRAILBLAZER

High on a knoll in the Pennsylvania back-woods in 1734, the small cabin was home to a Quaker family. It pleasured Squire and Sarah Boone that their sixth child was a boy. They named him Daniel.

Daniel's mother taught him to read, write, and cipher numbers. Spelling baffled Daniel, but he purely loved to read.

Daniel took to tracking and hunting in the woods with his Indian friends. In Daniel's twelfth year, his father gave him a long rifle. He became such an expert rifleman that folks said he could shoot a tick off a wildcat's nose from one hundred yards.

As homesteaders flocked to the Pennsylvania countryside, Daniel's father decided it was time to move his family to North Carolina. They needed elbowroom.

It was there in the Yadkin Valley that Daniel set his sights on Rebecca Bryan. They soon married and commenced housekeeping. By then, Daniel had gained a reputation as one of the country's best woodsmen.

Daniel often went on long hunts, sometimes alone and sometimes with three or four hunting companions. Days led to weeks, and weeks led to months that Daniel was gone.

During the hunts he carved messages in trees. He usually carved in beech trees because they had smooth bark and grew slowly. When he carved deeply, bark would not grow over the message. He used these carvings as boundary lines, guides for others to follow, and fun records of his journeys.

His carvings could be found far and wide. One tree bore the words, *D. Boon Cilled a bar on tree in the year 1760*. Another carving delivered the message, *D. Boon campt here.*

When he hunted in cold, wet weather, Daniel
found a good night's sleep in the comfort of a cave.

Sometimes on cool, frosty nights he curled up deep inside a bearskin or piled leaves around himself. Other times he cut bark from a tree and wrapped up in it to keep warm.

One day, when Daniel was back at home, an old friend, John Findley, paid the Boones a visit. The dust hadn't settled before they began talking about a place the Iroquois called "Kanta-ke." Findley told Daniel about woods filled with so much wild game that a hunter had to be careful not to get run over.

Daniel began to ponder ideas about the Kanta-ke wilderness. A wanderlust got under his skin and began to fester like a boil. When he could stand it no longer, Daniel headed out for Kentucky with his gun, Tick-Licker, and his favorite book, *Gulliver's Travels*.

Daniel journeyed on horseback. As he neared the gap of a mountain, Daniel felt the earth tremble. He heard a roar of thunder as plain as day. As he spied the clear, blue sky, his mind filled with wonderment. Then he saw the approaching storm. A thundering herd of buffalo stampeded across a far-flung, Kentucky grassland.

Daniel loved this wild land, so when Richard Henderson offered him the job of leading 30 huntsmen to Kentucky to cut a path, he obliged. On March 10, 1775, axes rang as Daniel and the men began blazing the 208-mile-long Wilderness Road.

By April 1, 1775, the woodsmen had cleared a path to the Kentucky River. Boone declared the meadow near the river the end of the Wilderness Road, and they built a fort. Daniel's pay for his work was two thousand acres of land and the naming of the fort, Fort Boonesborough, in his honor.

Daniel was ever mindful of the wild game around the fort and knew that without a good supply of meat, the people in the fort would not survive. He soon called a meeting to announce a law: no wasting of game.

A few weeks later Daniel returned home to North Carolina. There he found not only his family, but also, not more than fifty miles away, another family, which had built a cabin practically in the Boones' backyard. That's when Daniel told Rebecca they needed more elbowroom.

The Boone family set out for Fort Boonesborough. In a short time other families followed their lead and moved to the fort.

Life at Boonesborough was hard. Everybody worked; even the children helped plant gardens and raise crops.

Before long Daniel got wind of bad news. He did not have a legal title to the two thousand acres of land given to him for his work on the Wilderness Road. Disappointed, the Boone family headed westward, where new land brought new promise.

Daniel busied himself running a store and leading families into Kentucky to live. Even Abraham Lincoln's family followed Boone westward.

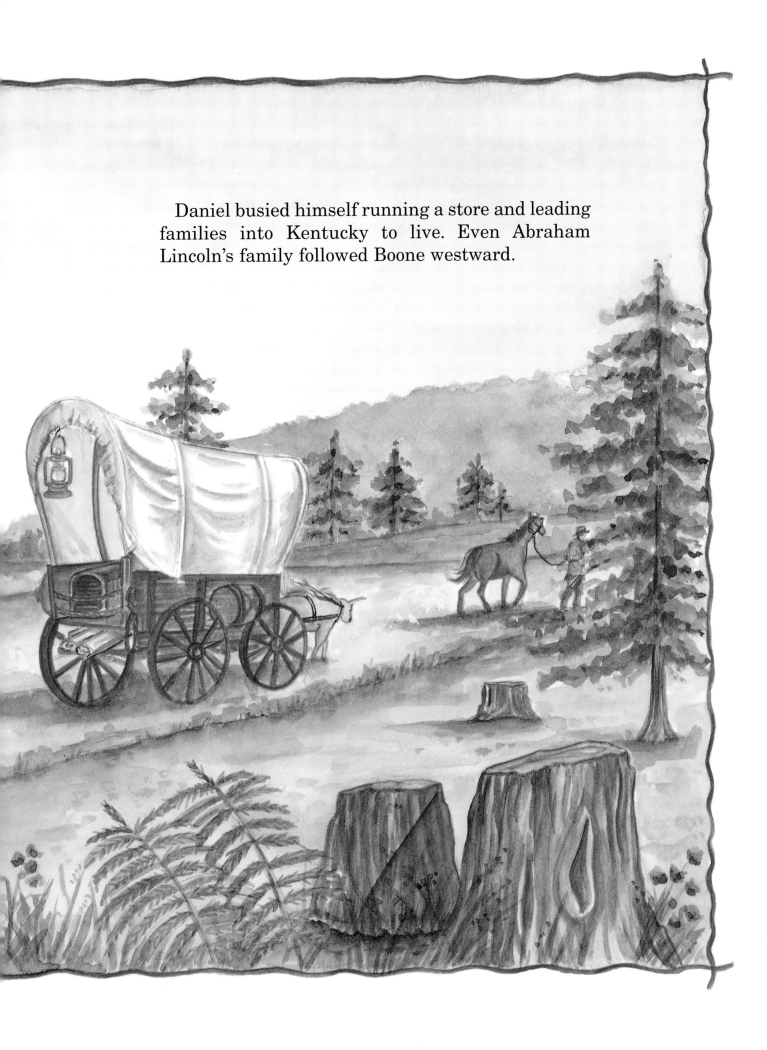

Daniel also surveyed land for people who staked claims. He and his sons used knives to carve boundary marks in the bark of trees. By 1781, Daniel Boone was one of the richest men in Kentucky. He had surveyed and claimed one hundred thousand acres of land. This was his reward for opening the West for settlement while receiving little or no pay. But the rewards were short lived.

A notch in a tree was often the only boundary mark Daniel made. However, a year's growth of bark can cover the carving, especially if the mark was carved in a tree with thick bark. When Daniel's marks were covered, other surveyors marked different boundaries and laid claim to the land.

Daniel lost his land in the courts. What land he didn't lose, he had to sell to pay off debts to the people who had hired him to survey. They, too, had lost their land.

Boone was no longer a landowner, but he had become famous. He worked with the legislature to make Kentucky a county of Virginia and later worked to make Kentucky a state. In 1798 a county was named Boone in his honor.

Disappointed that the forests were no longer great hunting grounds, Daniel headed farther west. He again needed elbowroom. He and Rebecca moved their family to Missouri, where Boone was given a tract of land. To satisfy his wandering nature, he explored new territory.

Bad luck with land deals seemed to follow Daniel no matter how often he moved or how far. In Missouri, Daniel once again lost land due to boundary claims.

One day when Daniel was in his eighties, a young man named Chester Harding called on him to paint his portrait. Harding asked Daniel if he had ever been lost, wandering alone in the forest for months at a time.

"No," Daniel declared, "I can't say I was ever lost, but I was bewildered once for three days."

Daniel and Rebecca lived out their lives in the Missouri wilderness. Daniel was content with many of his ten children living nearby and with a passel of grandchildren ever begging grandpa for just one more story about his days as a trailblazer.